BARNES
& NOBLE
B O O K S
NEW YORK

This edition published by Barnes & Noble, Inc.

10 9 8 7 6 5 4 3

ISBN 0-7607-2644-2

First published 2000

Stories and illustrations by Shirley Barber

Copyright © Marbit Pty Ltd

This anthology © The Five Mile Press Pty Ltd

This edition © 2001 Barnes & Noble Books

Printed in Singapore

Shirley Barber's

Let's Look at Colors

At the back of this book, there is a special color pallet showing the names of the colors featured in the illustrations.

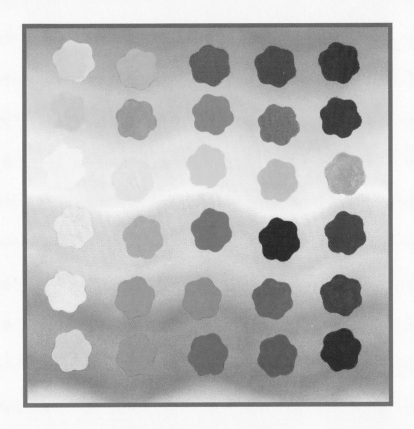

Children can use this pallet to help them identify the many different shades of color in each picture.

Shirley Barber's
Let's Look at Colors

BARNES
&NOBLE
B O O K S
N E W   Y O R K

These little workmice are painting
the toy fire engine red
What a mess they are making!

Let's look at the colors!
How many different shades of red
can you see?

The orange leaves are falling from
the trees and the frisky cats are playing with them.

Let's look at the colors!
How many different shades of orange
can you see?

Teddy and his sister Tiffany are
playing among the yellow buttercups.
Lots of butterflies are coming to say
"Hello!"

How many different shades of yellow
can you see?

Famous Professor Spot O'Doggarty has been searching for the rare green smiling Jungle Frog — and he's found it!

How many different shades of green can you see?

Princess Mewlinda
has gone to bed early to read her book.
You can tell that her favorite color is blue!

How many different shades of blue
can you see?

Queen Kitty loves gardening.
She is growing beautiful purple pansies
on the castle terrace.

How many different shades of purple
can you see?

These naughty kittens have pulled out
some balls of knitting wool.
The little pup is playing with the blue wool.

Let's look at all the colored wool.
How many different colors
can you see?

Pale Pink

Rose Pink

Primary Red

Poster Red

Crimson

Pale Orange

Orange

Vermillion

Burnt Orange

Sienna

Pale Yellow

Primrose

Primary Yellow

Cadmium Yellow

Yellow Ochre

Pale Green

Leaf Green

Viridian

BottleGreen

Olive Green

Pale Blue

Turquoise Blue

Sky Blue

Primary Blue

Ultramarine

Mauve

Light Violet

Dark Violet

Magenta

Imperial Purple

Queen Kitty loves gardening.
She is growing beautiful purple pansies
on the castle terrace.

How many different shades of purple
can you see?